Jr. Graphic African-American History

Frederick Douglass and the Abolitionist Movement

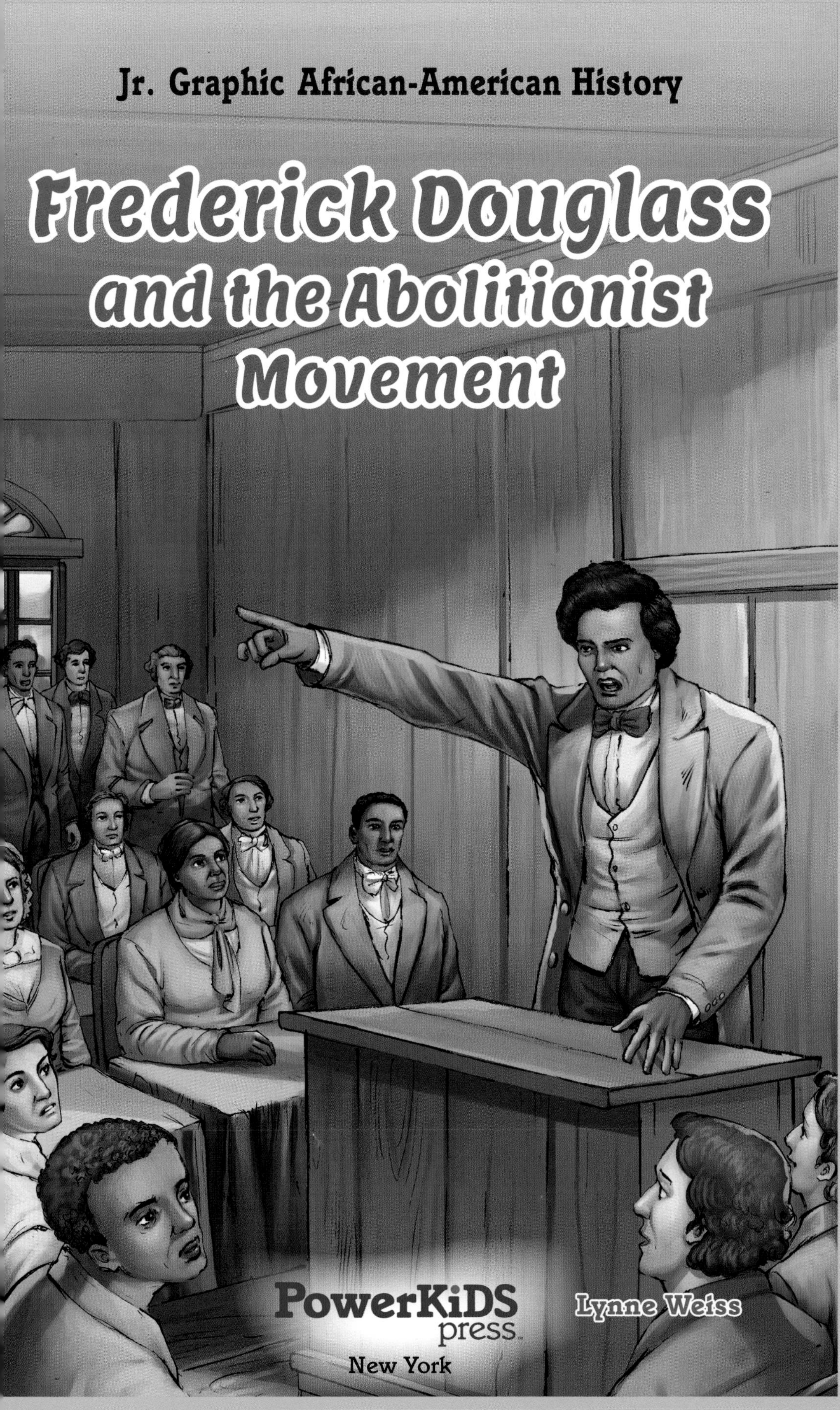

Lynne Weiss

PowerKiDS press
New York

Published in 2014 by The Rosen Publishing Group, Inc.
29 East 21st Street, New York, NY 10010

Copyright © 2014 by The Rosen Publishing Group, Inc.

All rights reserved. No part of this book may be reproduced in any form
without permission in writing from the publisher, except by a reviewer.

First Edition

Editor: Joanne Randolph

Book Design: Planman Technologies

Illustrations: Planman Technologies

Library of Congress Cataloging-in-Publication Data

Weiss, Lynne, 1952-

Frederick Douglass and the abolitionist movement / by Lynne Weiss. — First
edition.

pages cm. — (Jr. graphic African-American history)

Includes index.

ISBN 978-1-4777-1313-6 (library binding) — ISBN 978-1-4777-1451-5 (pbk.)
— ISBN 978-1-4777-1452-2 (6-pack)

1. Douglass, Frederick, 1818-1895—Juvenile literature. 2. Abolitionists—United
States—Biography—Juvenile literature. 3. African American abolitionists—
Biography—Juvenile literature. 4. Antislavery movements—United States—
Juvenile literature. 5. Douglass, Frederick, 1818-1895—Comic books, strips,
etc. 6. Abolitionists—United States—Biography—Comic books, strips, etc.
7. African American abolitionists—Biography—Comic books, strips, etc.
8. Antislavery movements—United State—Comic books, strips, etc.
9. Graphic novels. I. Title.

E449.D75W454 2014

973.8092—dc23

[B]

2012048609

Manufactured in the United States of America

CPSIA Compliance Information: Batch #S13PK1: For Further Information contact Rosen Publishing,
New York, New York at 1-800-237-9932

Contents

Introduction

Frederick Douglass was one of the greatest orators and writers of the **abolitionist movement**. Born into slavery in Maryland, he was determined to learn to read. Once he did, he was just as determined to become free. He escaped to the North, where he began to win fame for his public speaking and for his writing. He published his own newspaper, the *North Star*, and attended the first convention for women's rights in 1848 in Seneca Falls, New York. President Abraham Lincoln sought his advice, and Douglass encouraged northern African Americans to fight on the side of the Union in the Civil War. After the war, he continued to fight for equal rights for African Americans and women.

Main Characters

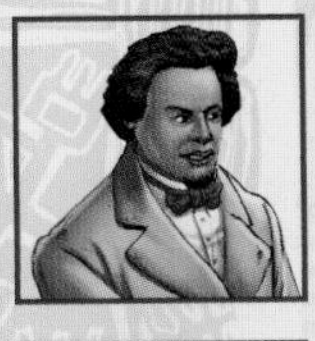

Frederick Douglass (1818–1895) African-American orator and writer.

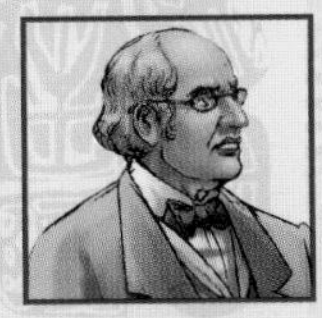

William Lloyd Garrison (1805–1879) Leading US abolitionist and editor of the *Liberator*. He was an early supporter of Douglass.

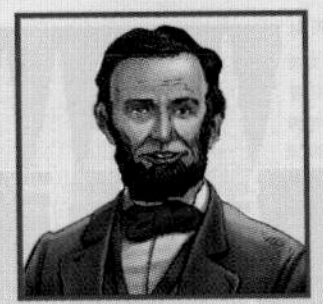

Abraham Lincoln (1809–1865) Sixteenth president of the United States. Lincoln led the Union to victory in the Civil War and ended slavery in the United States. He was assassinated just days after the end of the war.

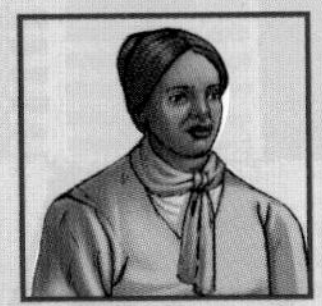

Anna Murray (1813–1882) First wife of Frederick Douglass.

FREDERICK DOUGLASS

IN AUGUST 1841, A YOUNG MAN NAMED FREDERICK DOUGLASS STOOD TO SPEAK AT AN ANTISLAVERY MEETING IN NANTUCKET, MASSACHUSETTS. HE WAS NERVOUS AT FIRST, BUT ONCE HE STARTED TO SPEAK, HIS STORY CAME EASILY.

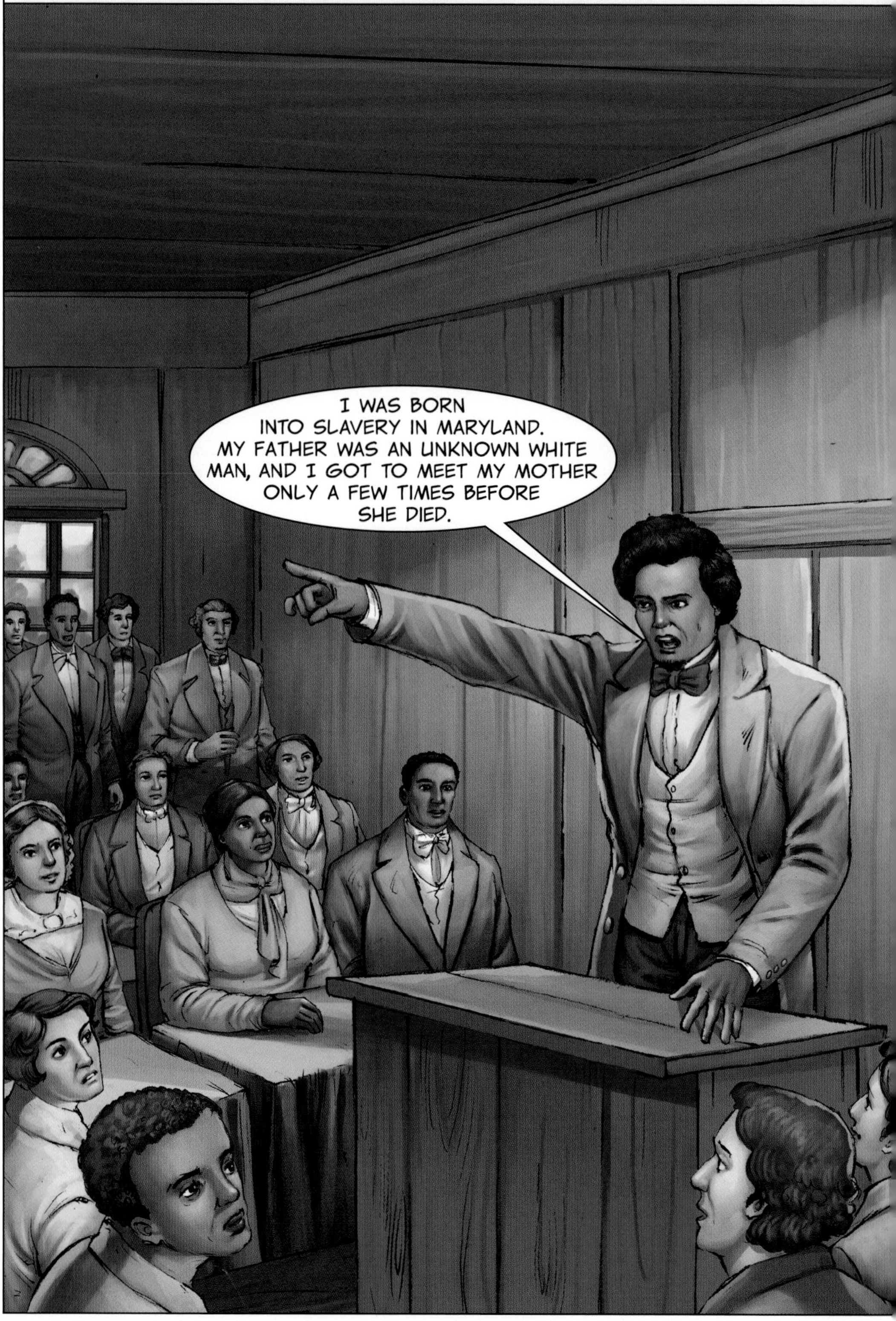
I WAS BORN INTO SLAVERY IN MARYLAND. MY FATHER WAS AN UNKNOWN WHITE MAN, AND I GOT TO MEET MY MOTHER ONLY A FEW TIMES BEFORE SHE DIED.

LEADING ABOLITIONISTS INCLUDING WENDELL PHILLIPS AND WILLIAM LLOYD GARRISON WERE AT THAT MEETING. THEY ASKED DOUGLASS IF HE WOULD BECOME A SPEAKER FOR THE ANTISLAVERY SOCIETY.

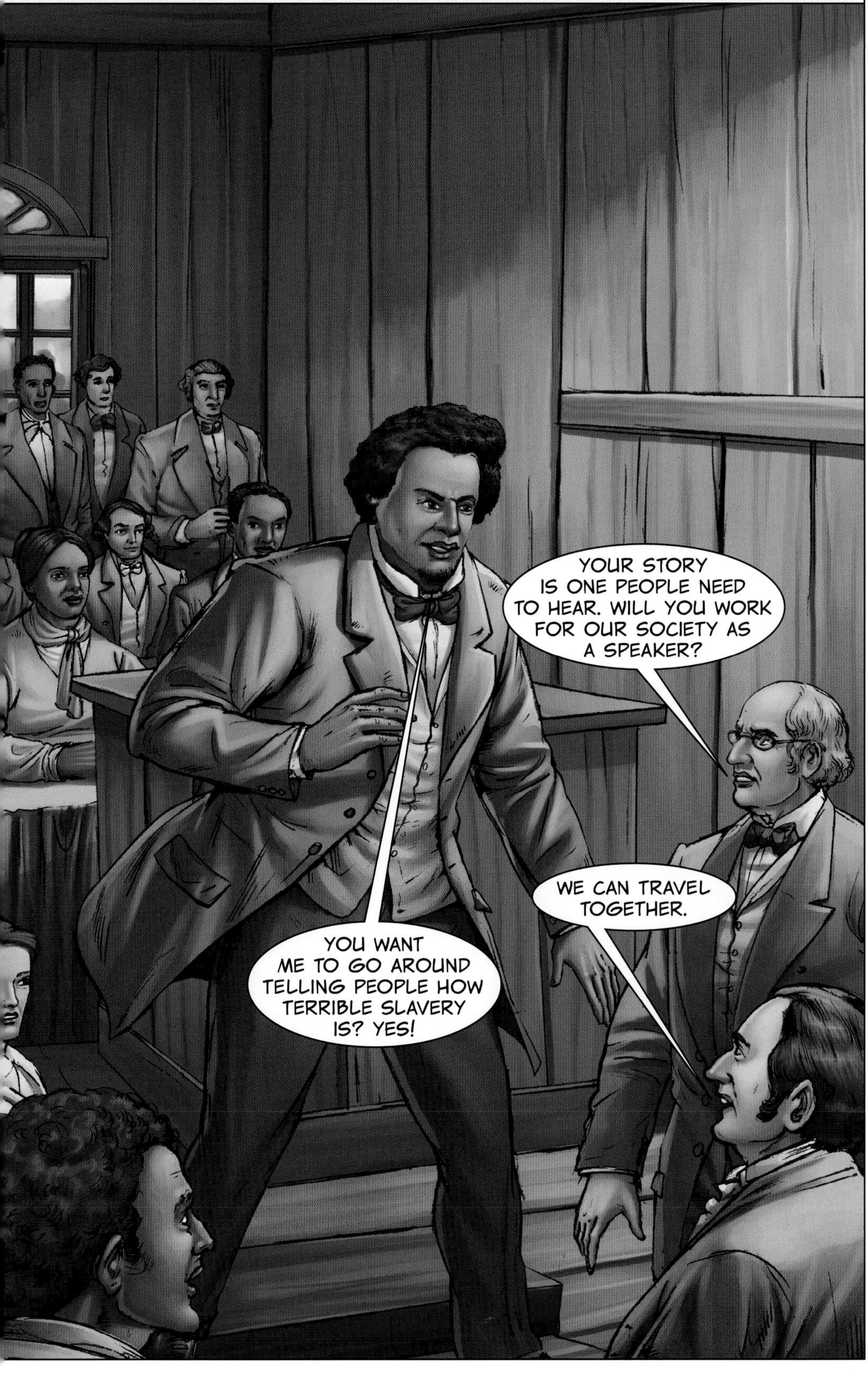
YOUR STORY IS ONE PEOPLE NEED TO HEAR. WILL YOU WORK FOR OUR SOCIETY AS A SPEAKER?
YOU WANT ME TO GO AROUND TELLING PEOPLE HOW TERRIBLE SLAVERY IS? YES!
WE CAN TRAVEL TOGETHER.

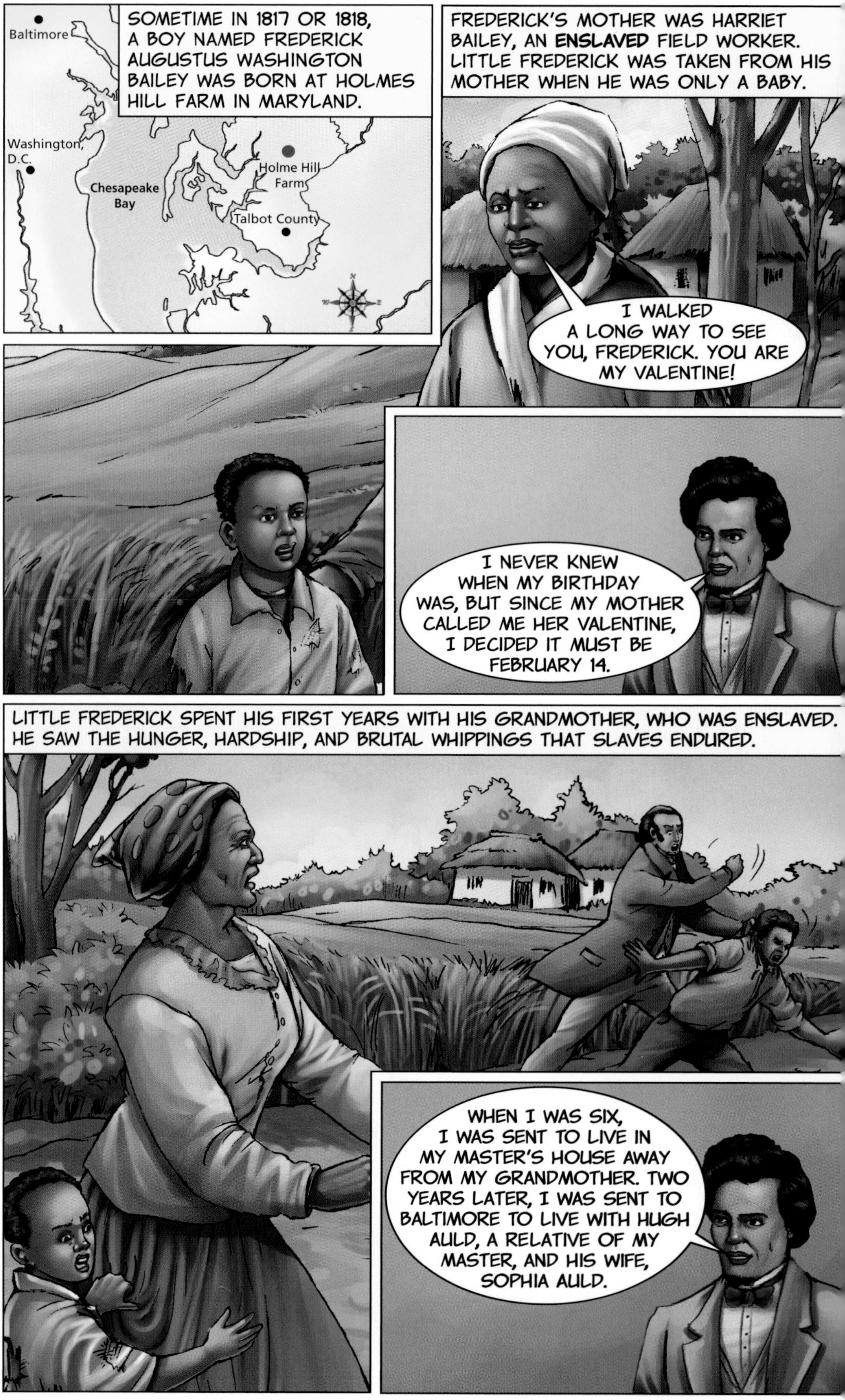

SOMETIME IN 1817 OR 1818, A BOY NAMED FREDERICK AUGUSTUS WASHINGTON BAILEY WAS BORN AT HOLMES HILL FARM IN MARYLAND.
Baltimore
Washington, D.C.
Chesapeake Bay
Holme Hill Farm
Talbot County
FREDERICK'S MOTHER WAS HARRIET BAILEY, AN **ENSLAVED** FIELD WORKER. LITTLE FREDERICK WAS TAKEN FROM HIS MOTHER WHEN HE WAS ONLY A BABY.
I WALKED A LONG WAY TO SEE YOU, FREDERICK. YOU ARE MY VALENTINE!
I NEVER KNEW WHEN MY BIRTHDAY WAS, BUT SINCE MY MOTHER CALLED ME HER VALENTINE, I DECIDED IT MUST BE FEBRUARY 14.
LITTLE FREDERICK SPENT HIS FIRST YEARS WITH HIS GRANDMOTHER, WHO WAS ENSLAVED. HE SAW THE HUNGER, HARDSHIP, AND BRUTAL WHIPPINGS THAT SLAVES ENDURED.
WHEN I WAS SIX, I WAS SENT TO LIVE IN MY MASTER'S HOUSE AWAY FROM MY GRANDMOTHER. TWO YEARS LATER, I WAS SENT TO BALTIMORE TO LIVE WITH HUGH AULD, A RELATIVE OF MY MASTER, AND HIS WIFE, SOPHIA AULD.

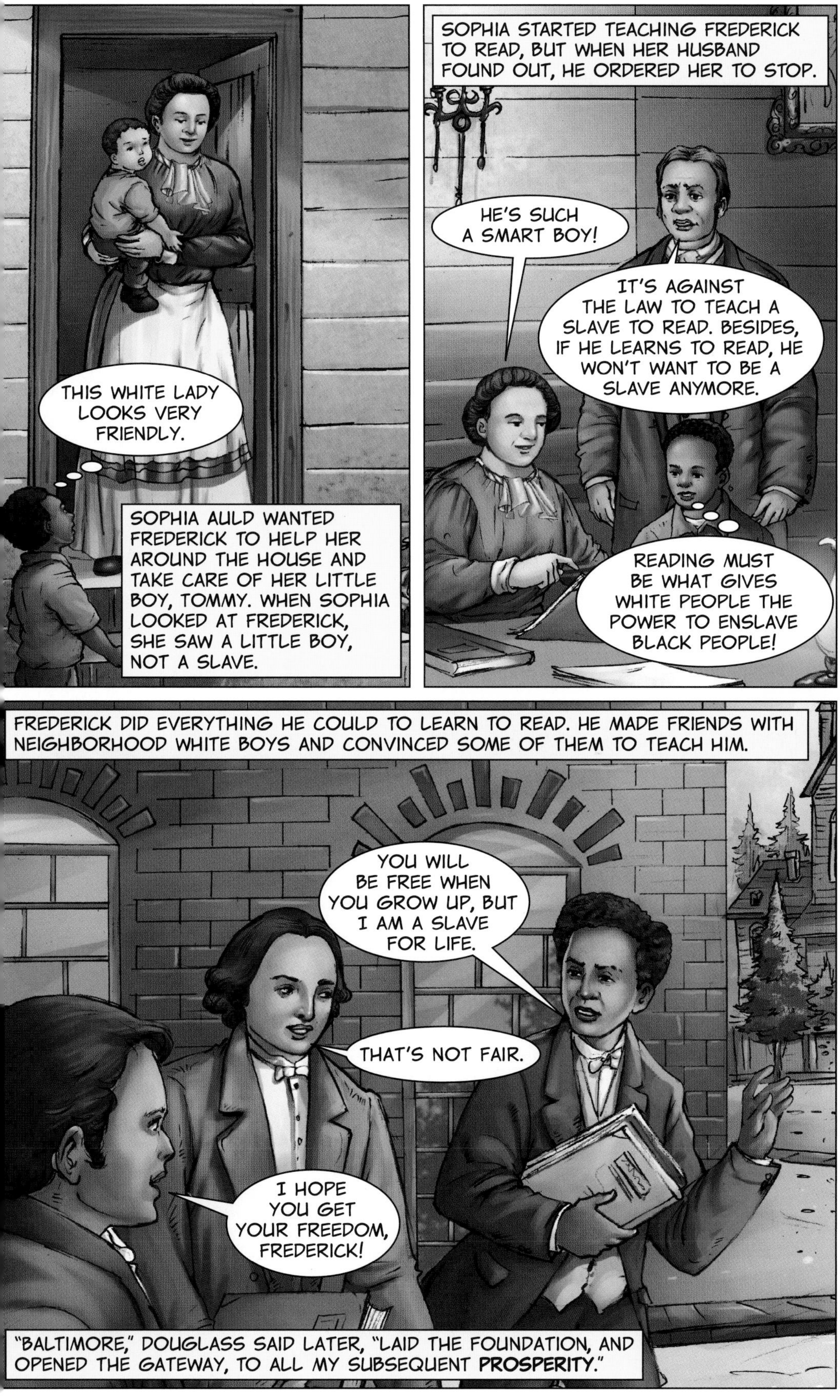
THIS WHITE LADY LOOKS VERY FRIENDLY.
SOPHIA AULD WANTED FREDERICK TO HELP HER AROUND THE HOUSE AND TAKE CARE OF HER LITTLE BOY, TOMMY. WHEN SOPHIA LOOKED AT FREDERICK, SHE SAW A LITTLE BOY, NOT A SLAVE.
SOPHIA STARTED TEACHING FREDERICK TO READ, BUT WHEN HER HUSBAND FOUND OUT, HE ORDERED HER TO STOP.
HE'S SUCH A SMART BOY!
IT'S AGAINST THE LAW TO TEACH A SLAVE TO READ. BESIDES, IF HE LEARNS TO READ, HE WON'T WANT TO BE A SLAVE ANYMORE.
READING MUST BE WHAT GIVES WHITE PEOPLE THE POWER TO ENSLAVE BLACK PEOPLE!
FREDERICK DID EVERYTHING HE COULD TO LEARN TO READ. HE MADE FRIENDS WITH NEIGHBORHOOD WHITE BOYS AND CONVINCED SOME OF THEM TO TEACH HIM.
YOU WILL BE FREE WHEN YOU GROW UP, BUT I AM A SLAVE FOR LIFE.
THAT'S NOT FAIR.
I HOPE YOU GET YOUR FREEDOM, FREDERICK!
"BALTIMORE," DOUGLASS SAID LATER, "LAID THE FOUNDATION, AND OPENED THE GATEWAY, TO ALL MY SUBSEQUENT **PROSPERITY**."

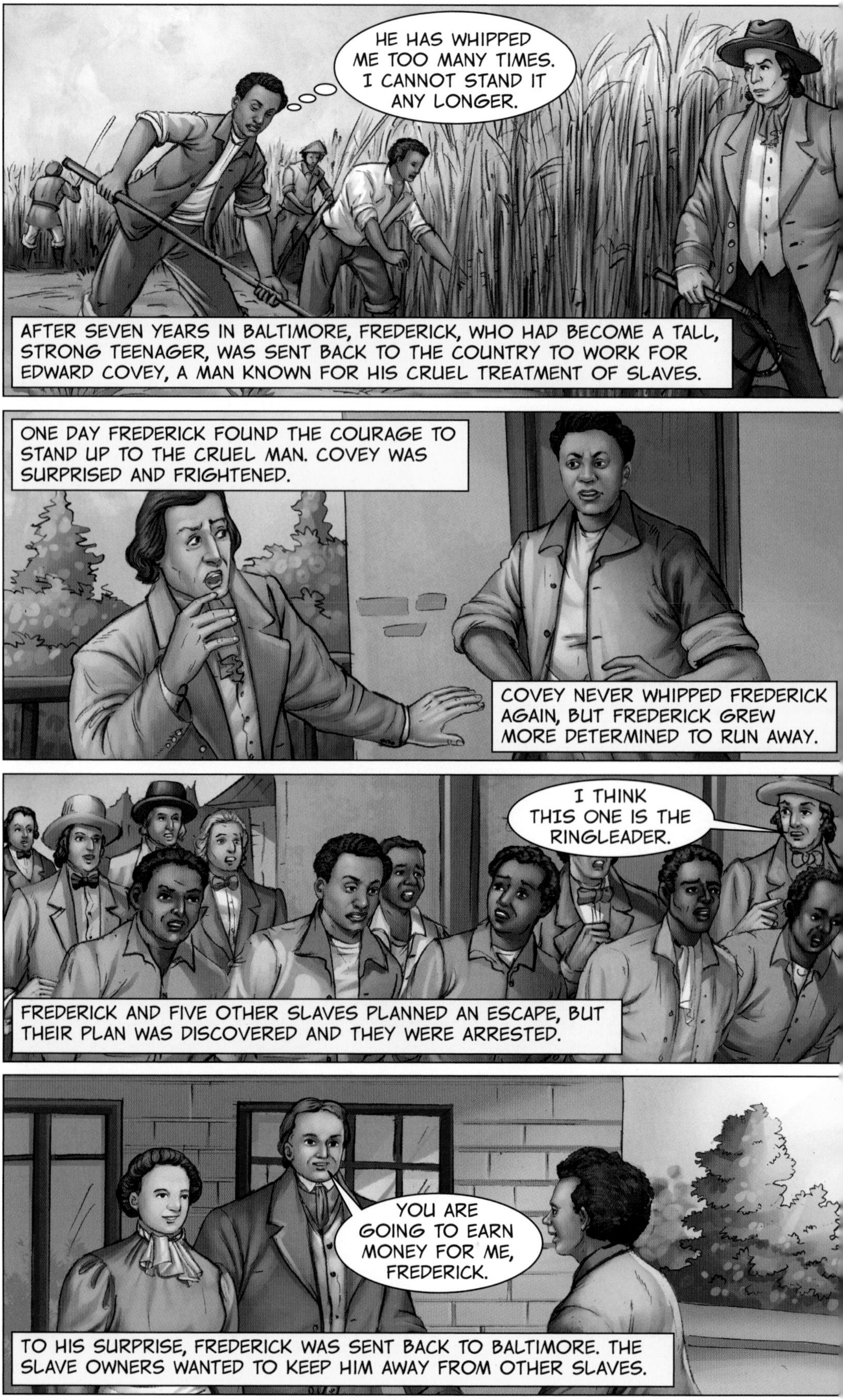
HE HAS WHIPPED ME TOO MANY TIMES. I CANNOT STAND IT ANY LONGER.
AFTER SEVEN YEARS IN BALTIMORE, FREDERICK, WHO HAD BECOME A TALL, STRONG TEENAGER, WAS SENT BACK TO THE COUNTRY TO WORK FOR EDWARD COVEY, A MAN KNOWN FOR HIS CRUEL TREATMENT OF SLAVES.
ONE DAY FREDERICK FOUND THE COURAGE TO STAND UP TO THE CRUEL MAN. COVEY WAS SURPRISED AND FRIGHTENED.
COVEY NEVER WHIPPED FREDERICK AGAIN, BUT FREDERICK GREW MORE DETERMINED TO RUN AWAY.
I THINK THIS ONE IS THE RINGLEADER.
FREDERICK AND FIVE OTHER SLAVES PLANNED AN ESCAPE, BUT THEIR PLAN WAS DISCOVERED AND THEY WERE ARRESTED.
YOU ARE GOING TO EARN MONEY FOR ME, FREDERICK.
TO HIS SURPRISE, FREDERICK WAS SENT BACK TO BALTIMORE. THE SLAVE OWNERS WANTED TO KEEP HIM AWAY FROM OTHER SLAVES.

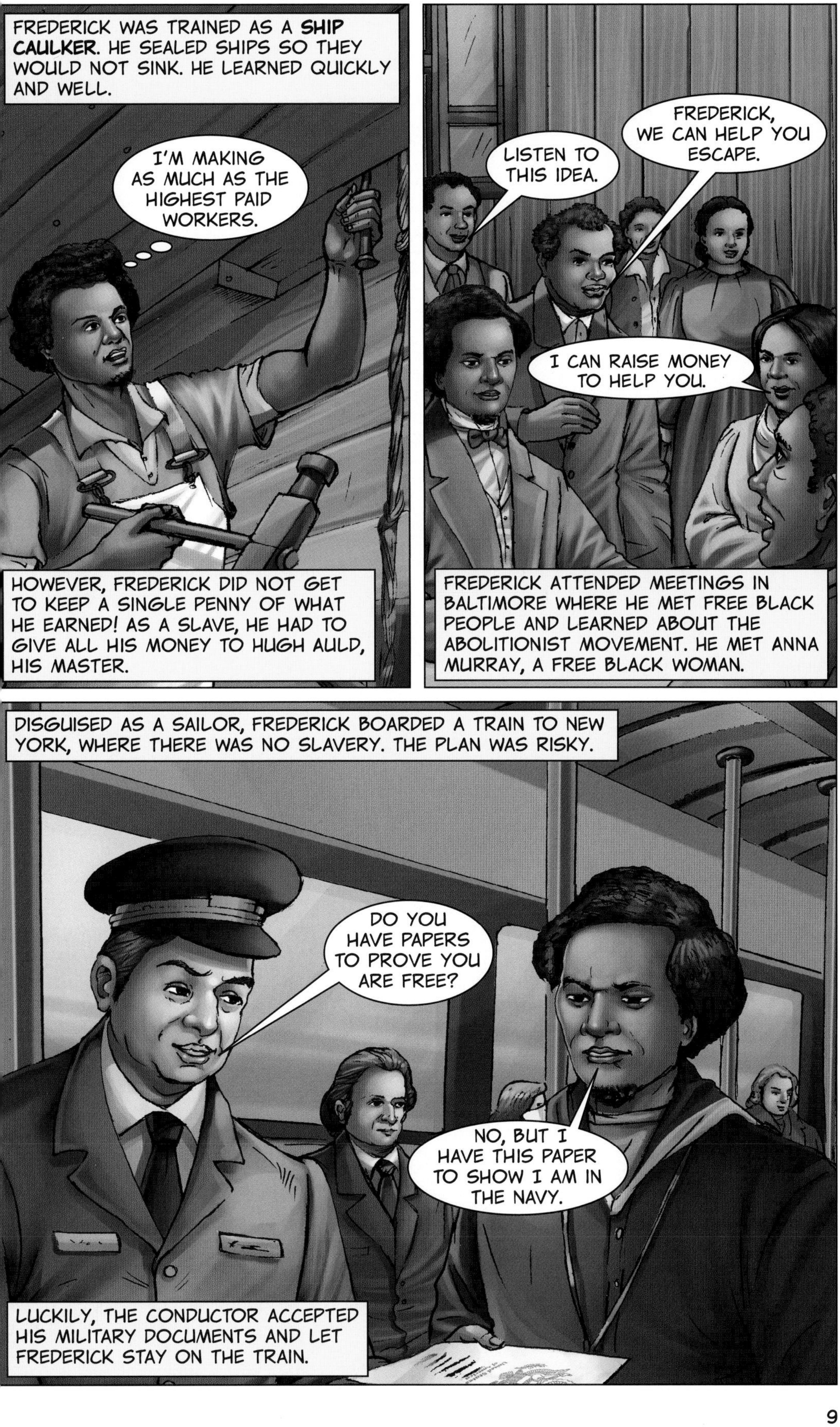
FREDERICK WAS TRAINED AS A **SHIP CAULKER**. HE SEALED SHIPS SO THEY WOULD NOT SINK. HE LEARNED QUICKLY AND WELL.
I'M MAKING AS MUCH AS THE HIGHEST PAID WORKERS.
HOWEVER, FREDERICK DID NOT GET TO KEEP A SINGLE PENNY OF WHAT HE EARNED! AS A SLAVE, HE HAD TO GIVE ALL HIS MONEY TO HUGH AULD, HIS MASTER.
LISTEN TO THIS IDEA.
FREDERICK, WE CAN HELP YOU ESCAPE.
I CAN RAISE MONEY TO HELP YOU.
FREDERICK ATTENDED MEETINGS IN BALTIMORE WHERE HE MET FREE BLACK PEOPLE AND LEARNED ABOUT THE ABOLITIONIST MOVEMENT. HE MET ANNA MURRAY, A FREE BLACK WOMAN.
DISGUISED AS A SAILOR, FREDERICK BOARDED A TRAIN TO NEW YORK, WHERE THERE WAS NO SLAVERY. THE PLAN WAS RISKY.
DO YOU HAVE PAPERS TO PROVE YOU ARE FREE?
NO, BUT I HAVE THIS PAPER TO SHOW I AM IN THE NAVY.
LUCKILY, THE CONDUCTOR ACCEPTED HIS MILITARY DOCUMENTS AND LET FREDERICK STAY ON THE TRAIN.

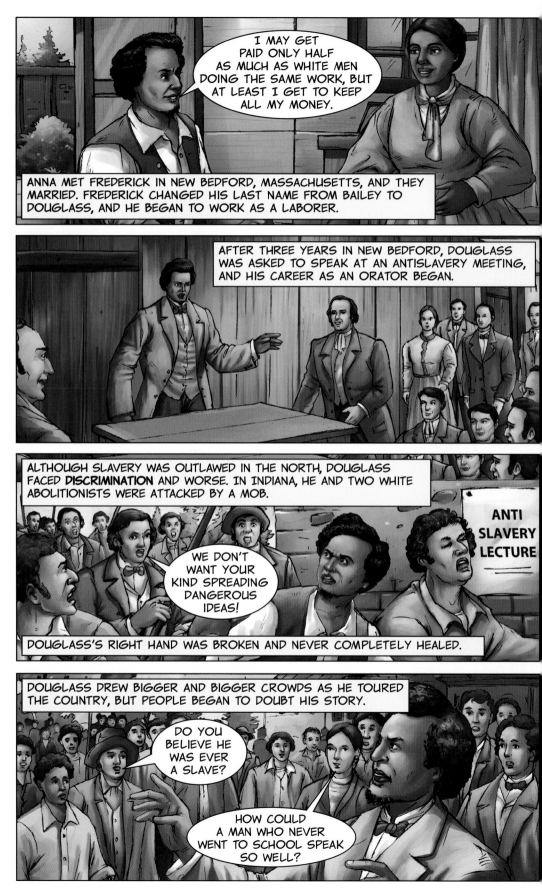

I MAY GET PAID ONLY HALF AS MUCH AS WHITE MEN DOING THE SAME WORK, BUT AT LEAST I GET TO KEEP ALL MY MONEY.

ANNA MET FREDERICK IN NEW BEDFORD, MASSACHUSETTS, AND THEY MARRIED. FREDERICK CHANGED HIS LAST NAME FROM BAILEY TO DOUGLASS, AND HE BEGAN TO WORK AS A LABORER.

AFTER THREE YEARS IN NEW BEDFORD, DOUGLASS WAS ASKED TO SPEAK AT AN ANTISLAVERY MEETING, AND HIS CAREER AS AN ORATOR BEGAN.

ALTHOUGH SLAVERY WAS OUTLAWED IN THE NORTH, DOUGLASS FACED **DISCRIMINATION** AND WORSE. IN INDIANA, HE AND TWO WHITE ABOLITIONISTS WERE ATTACKED BY A MOB.

WE DON'T WANT YOUR KIND SPREADING DANGEROUS IDEAS!

ANTI SLAVERY LECTURE

DOUGLASS'S RIGHT HAND WAS BROKEN AND NEVER COMPLETELY HEALED.

DOUGLASS DREW BIGGER AND BIGGER CROWDS AS HE TOURED THE COUNTRY, BUT PEOPLE BEGAN TO DOUBT HIS STORY.

DO YOU BELIEVE HE WAS EVER A SLAVE?

HOW COULD A MAN WHO NEVER WENT TO SCHOOL SPEAK SO WELL?

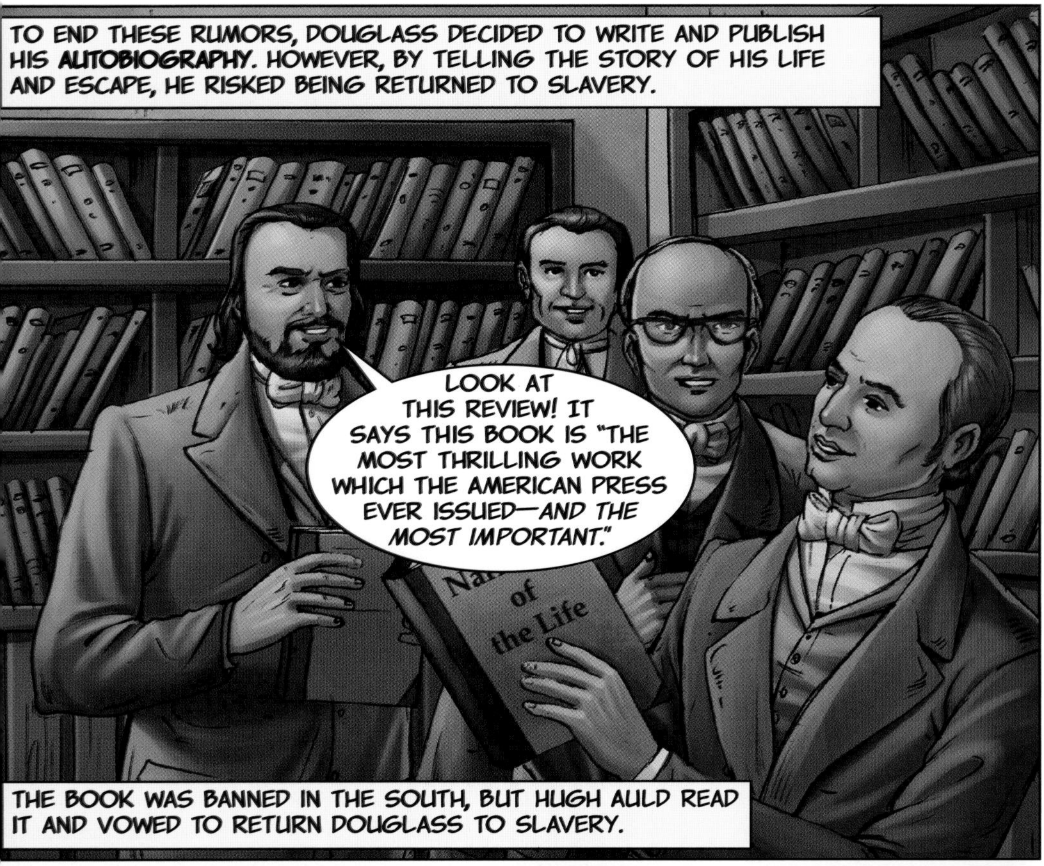
TO END THESE RUMORS, DOUGLASS DECIDED TO WRITE AND PUBLISH HIS **AUTOBIOGRAPHY**. HOWEVER, BY TELLING THE STORY OF HIS LIFE AND ESCAPE, HE RISKED BEING RETURNED TO SLAVERY.
LOOK AT THIS REVIEW! IT SAYS THIS BOOK IS "THE MOST THRILLING WORK WHICH THE AMERICAN PRESS EVER ISSUED—AND THE *MOST IMPORTANT*."
THE BOOK WAS BANNED IN THE SOUTH, BUT HUGH AULD READ IT AND VOWED TO RETURN DOUGLASS TO SLAVERY.

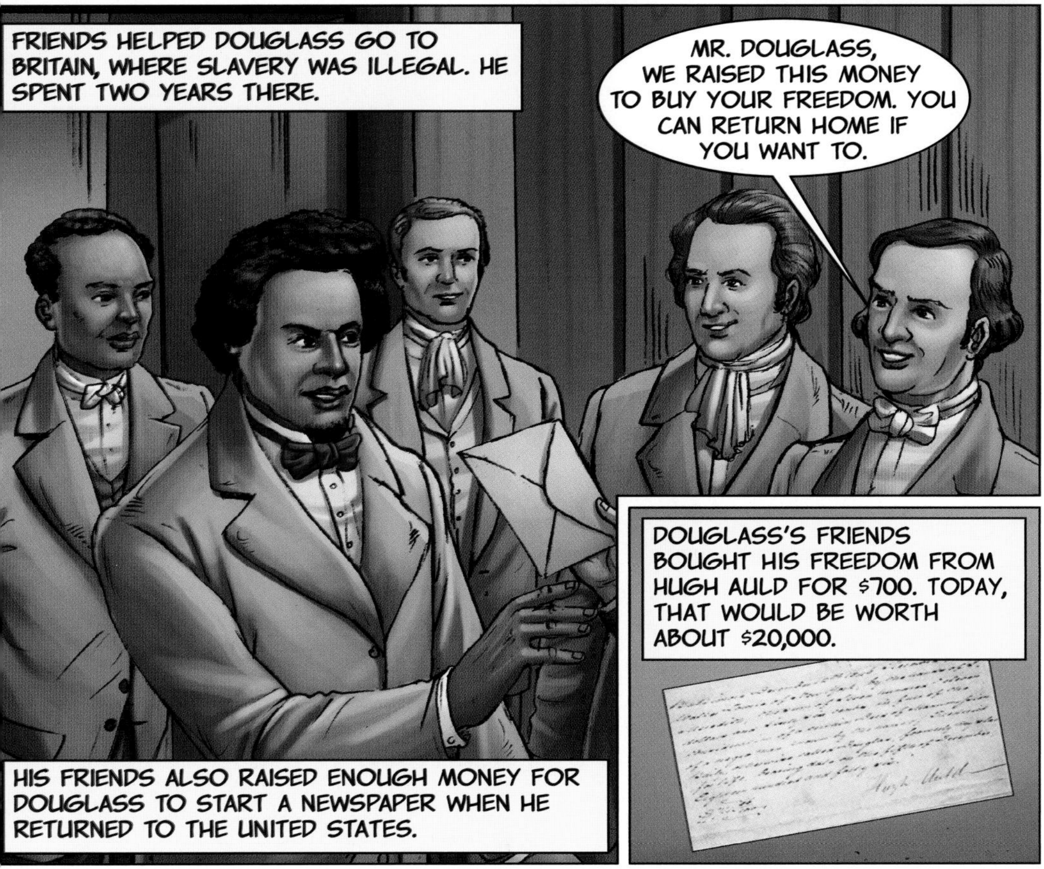
FRIENDS HELPED DOUGLASS GO TO BRITAIN, WHERE SLAVERY WAS ILLEGAL. HE SPENT TWO YEARS THERE.
MR. DOUGLASS, WE RAISED THIS MONEY TO BUY YOUR FREEDOM. YOU CAN RETURN HOME IF YOU WANT TO.
DOUGLASS'S FRIENDS BOUGHT HIS FREEDOM FROM HUGH AULD FOR $700. TODAY, THAT WOULD BE WORTH ABOUT $20,000.
HIS FRIENDS ALSO RAISED ENOUGH MONEY FOR DOUGLASS TO START A NEWSPAPER WHEN HE RETURNED TO THE UNITED STATES.

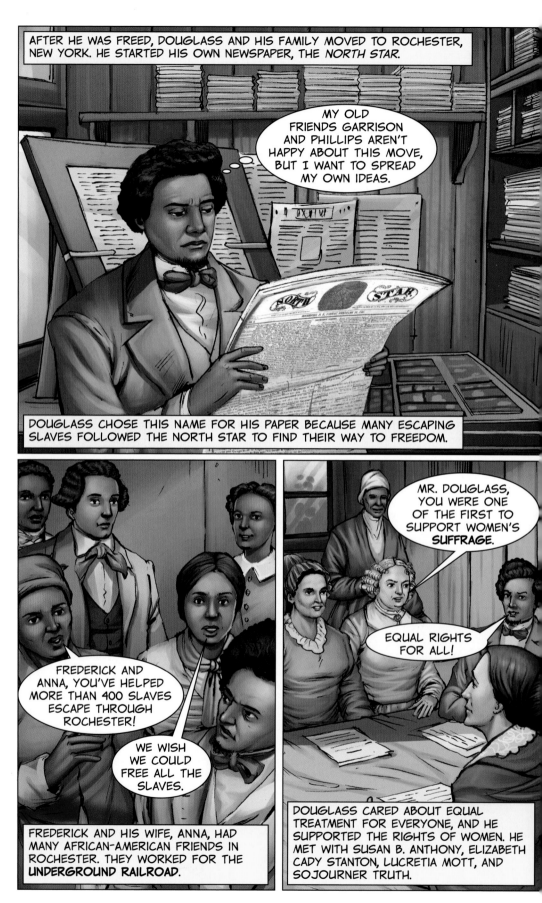

AFTER HE WAS FREED, DOUGLASS AND HIS FAMILY MOVED TO ROCHESTER, NEW YORK. HE STARTED HIS OWN NEWSPAPER, THE *NORTH STAR*.

MY OLD FRIENDS GARRISON AND PHILLIPS AREN'T HAPPY ABOUT THIS MOVE, BUT I WANT TO SPREAD MY OWN IDEAS.

DOUGLASS CHOSE THIS NAME FOR HIS PAPER BECAUSE MANY ESCAPING SLAVES FOLLOWED THE NORTH STAR TO FIND THEIR WAY TO FREEDOM.

FREDERICK AND ANNA, YOU'VE HELPED MORE THAN 400 SLAVES ESCAPE THROUGH ROCHESTER!

WE WISH WE COULD FREE ALL THE SLAVES.

FREDERICK AND HIS WIFE, ANNA, HAD MANY AFRICAN-AMERICAN FRIENDS IN ROCHESTER. THEY WORKED FOR THE **UNDERGROUND RAILROAD**.

MR. DOUGLASS, YOU WERE ONE OF THE FIRST TO SUPPORT WOMEN'S **SUFFRAGE**.

EQUAL RIGHTS FOR ALL!

DOUGLASS CARED ABOUT EQUAL TREATMENT FOR EVERYONE, AND HE SUPPORTED THE RIGHTS OF WOMEN. HE MET WITH SUSAN B. ANTHONY, ELIZABETH CADY STANTON, LUCRETIA MOTT, AND SOJOURNER TRUTH.

DOUGLASS GREW CLOSER TO NEW YORK ABOLITIONIST GERRIT SMITH, WHO DISAGREED WITH BOSTON ABOLITIONIST WILLIAM LLOYD GARRISON. SMITH WANTED TO USE ELECTIONS TO END SLAVERY. GARRISON DID NOT BELIEVE THIS WAS POSSIBLE.

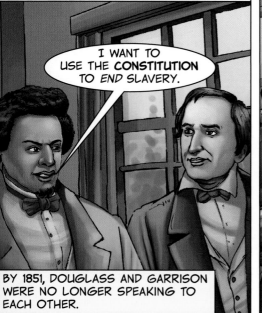

I WANT TO USE THE **CONSTITUTION** TO *END* SLAVERY.

BY 1851, DOUGLASS AND GARRISON WERE NO LONGER SPEAKING TO EACH OTHER.

IN THE SPRING OF 1860, DOUGLASS CAMPAIGNED FOR ABRAHAM LINCOLN, WHO PROMISED TO LIMIT THE SPREAD OF SLAVERY IF ELECTED PRESIDENT.

VOTE FOR ABE!

LINCOLN WON THE ELECTION. SLAVE-HOLDING STATES STARTED TO **SECEDE** AND FORM THE CONFEDERATE STATES OF AMERICA.

ON APRIL 12, 1861, CONFEDERATE TROOPS FIRED ON UNION TROOPS AT FORT SUMTER, JUST OUTSIDE OF CHARLESTON, SOUTH CAROLINA. THE CIVIL WAR HAD STARTED.

THIS WAR IS THE CHANCE TO DESTROY SLAVERY.

LATEST NEWS
By Telegraph to The Press.
WAR BEGUN!
FIRE OPENED ON FORT SUMTER

MOST PEOPLE THOUGHT THE WAR WOULD BE SHORT AND THAT THE UNION WOULD WIN.

THE NORTH HAD 23 STATES AND 22 MILLION PEOPLE LIVING IN THEM, ALONG WITH MOST OF THE NATION'S FACTORIES AND RAILROADS. THE SOUTH HAD ONLY 11 STATES AND 9 MILLION PEOPLE.

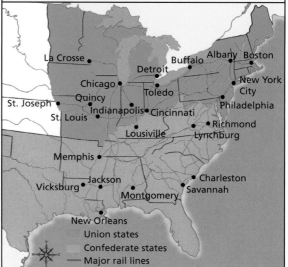

La Crosse
Detroit
Buffalo
Albany
Boston
Chicago
Toledo
New York City
St. Joseph
Quincy
Indianapolis
Cincinnati
Philadelphia
St. Louis
Lousiville
Richmond
Lynchburg
Memphis
Vicksburg
Jackson
Charleston
Savannah
Montgomery
New Orleans
Union states
Confederate states
Major rail lines

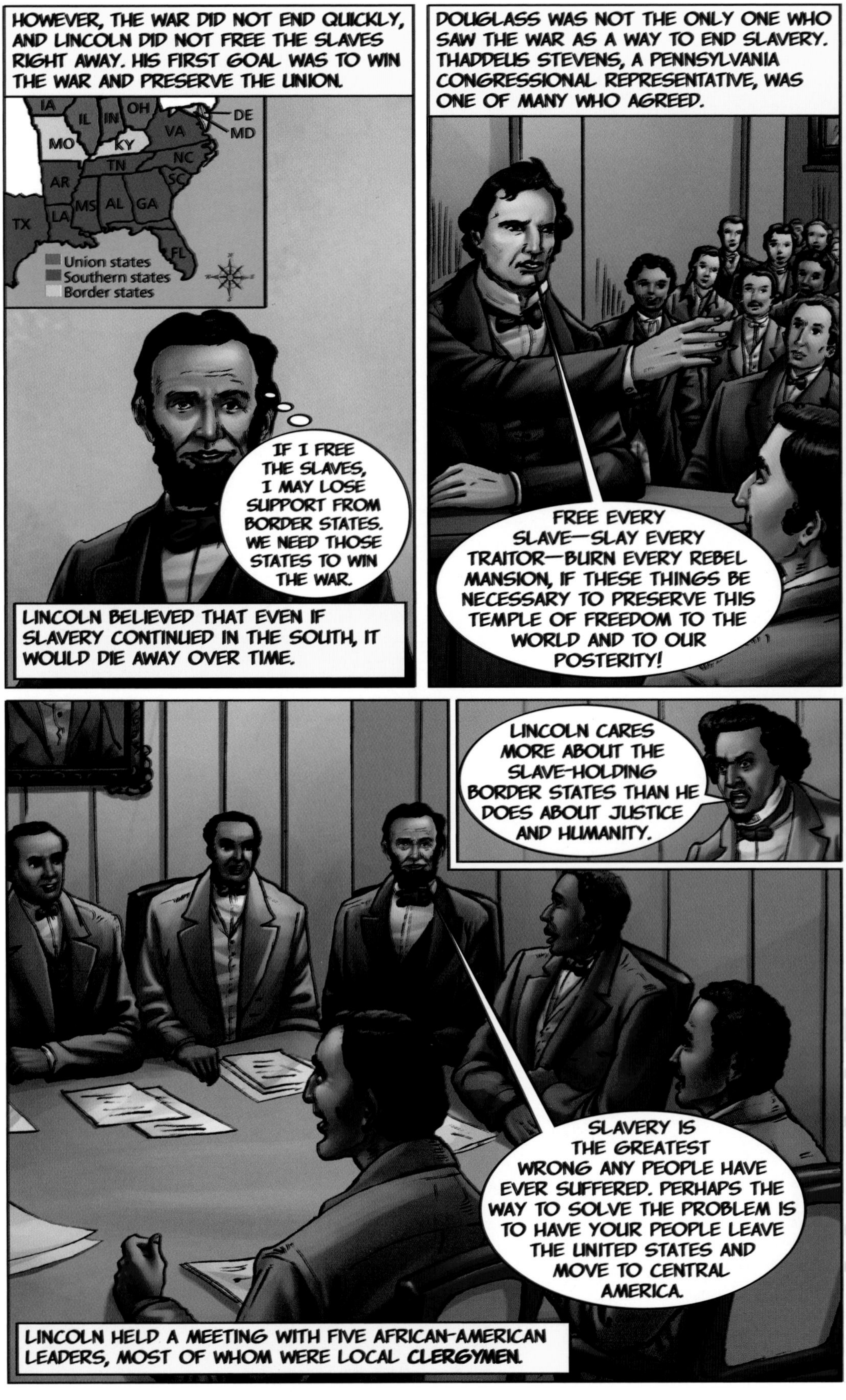
HOWEVER, THE WAR DID NOT END QUICKLY, AND LINCOLN DID NOT FREE THE SLAVES RIGHT AWAY. HIS FIRST GOAL WAS TO WIN THE WAR AND PRESERVE THE UNION.
IA IL IN OH DE MD MO KY VA TN NC AR SC MS AL GA LA TX FL
Union states
Southern states
Border states
IF I FREE THE SLAVES, I MAY LOSE SUPPORT FROM BORDER STATES. WE NEED THOSE STATES TO WIN THE WAR.
LINCOLN BELIEVED THAT EVEN IF SLAVERY CONTINUED IN THE SOUTH, IT WOULD DIE AWAY OVER TIME.
DOUGLASS WAS NOT THE ONLY ONE WHO SAW THE WAR AS A WAY TO END SLAVERY. THADDEUS STEVENS, A PENNSYLVANIA CONGRESSIONAL REPRESENTATIVE, WAS ONE OF MANY WHO AGREED.
FREE EVERY SLAVE—SLAY EVERY TRAITOR—BURN EVERY REBEL MANSION, IF THESE THINGS BE NECESSARY TO PRESERVE THIS TEMPLE OF FREEDOM TO THE WORLD AND TO OUR POSTERITY!
LINCOLN CARES MORE ABOUT THE SLAVE-HOLDING BORDER STATES THAN HE DOES ABOUT JUSTICE AND HUMANITY.
SLAVERY IS THE GREATEST WRONG ANY PEOPLE HAVE EVER SUFFERED. PERHAPS THE WAY TO SOLVE THE PROBLEM IS TO HAVE YOUR PEOPLE LEAVE THE UNITED STATES AND MOVE TO CENTRAL AMERICA.
LINCOLN HELD A MEETING WITH FIVE AFRICAN-AMERICAN LEADERS, MOST OF WHOM WERE LOCAL CLERGYMEN.

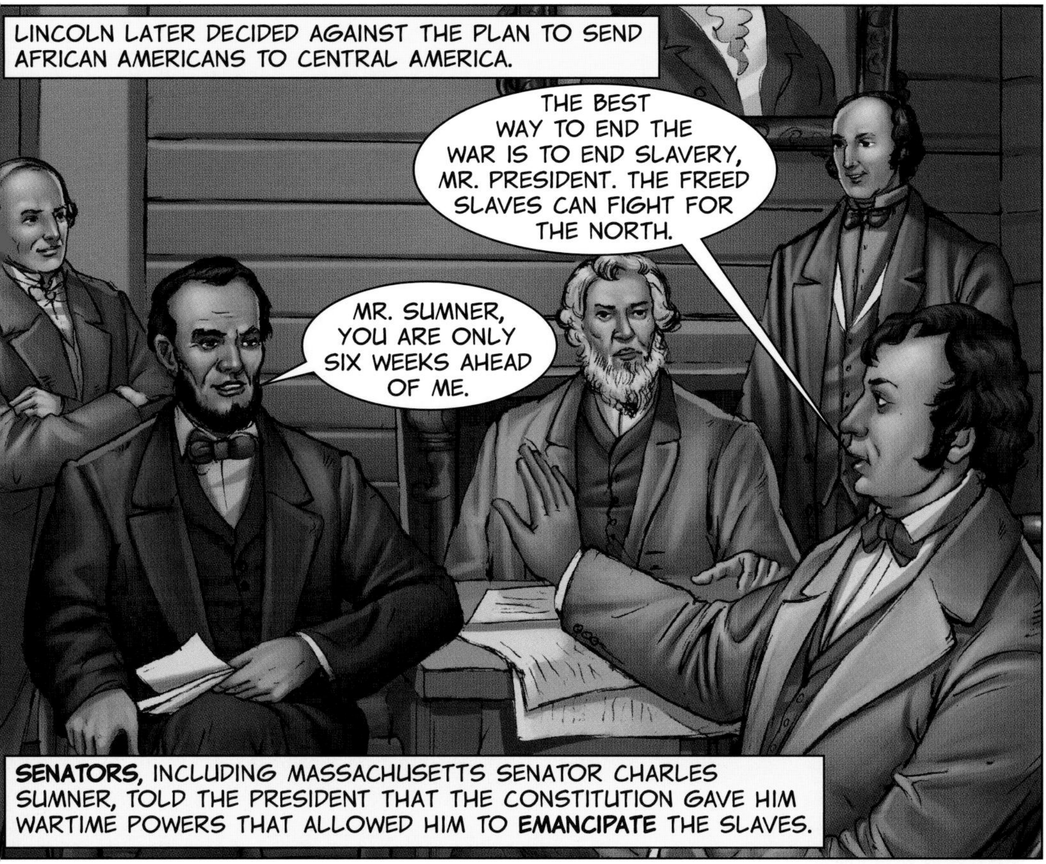
LINCOLN LATER DECIDED AGAINST THE PLAN TO SEND AFRICAN AMERICANS TO CENTRAL AMERICA.
THE BEST WAY TO END THE WAR IS TO END SLAVERY, MR. PRESIDENT. THE FREED SLAVES CAN FIGHT FOR THE NORTH.
MR. SUMNER, YOU ARE ONLY SIX WEEKS AHEAD OF ME.
SENATORS, INCLUDING MASSACHUSETTS SENATOR CHARLES SUMNER, TOLD THE PRESIDENT THAT THE CONSTITUTION GAVE HIM WARTIME POWERS THAT ALLOWED HIM TO **EMANCIPATE** THE SLAVES.

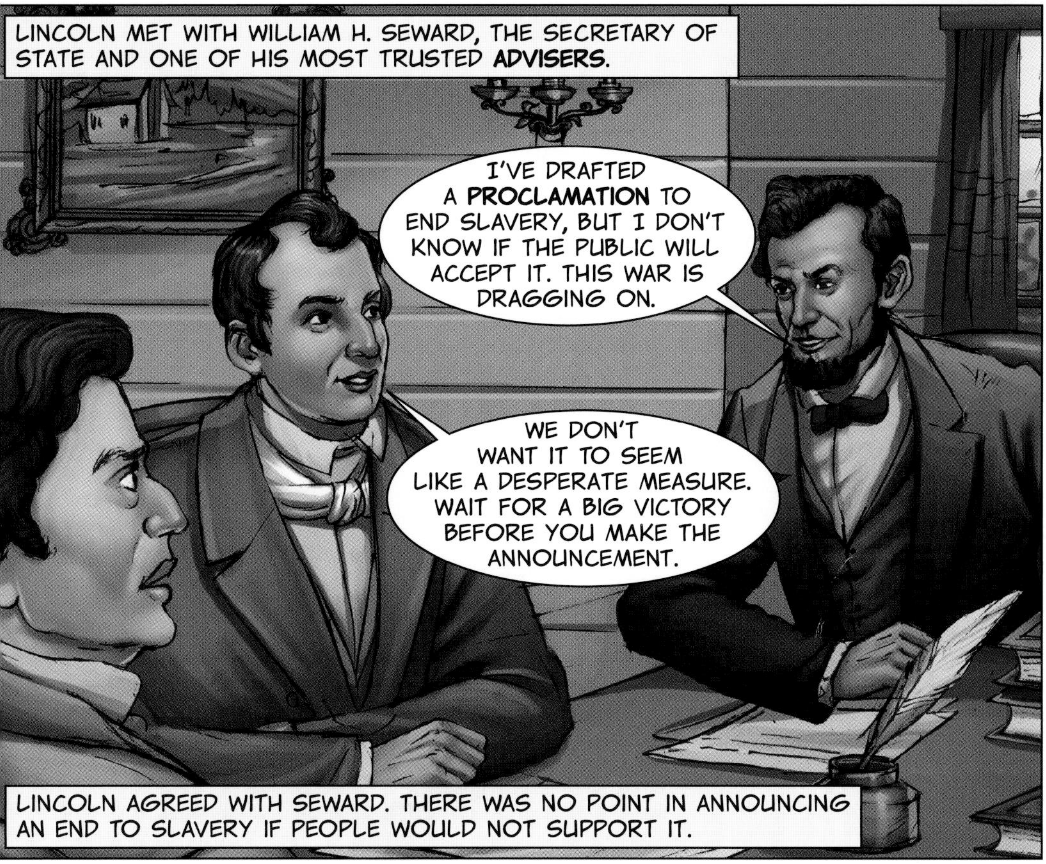
LINCOLN MET WITH WILLIAM H. SEWARD, THE SECRETARY OF STATE AND ONE OF HIS MOST TRUSTED **ADVISERS**.
I'VE DRAFTED A **PROCLAMATION** TO END SLAVERY, BUT I DON'T KNOW IF THE PUBLIC WILL ACCEPT IT. THIS WAR IS DRAGGING ON.
WE DON'T WANT IT TO SEEM LIKE A DESPERATE MEASURE. WAIT FOR A BIG VICTORY BEFORE YOU MAKE THE ANNOUNCEMENT.
LINCOLN AGREED WITH SEWARD. THERE WAS NO POINT IN ANNOUNCING AN END TO SLAVERY IF PEOPLE WOULD NOT SUPPORT IT.

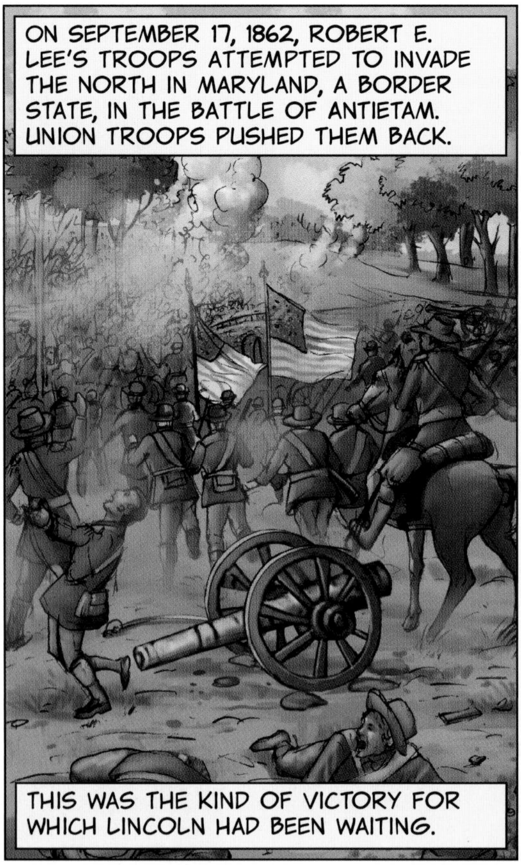
ON SEPTEMBER 17, 1862, ROBERT E. LEE'S TROOPS ATTEMPTED TO INVADE THE NORTH IN MARYLAND, A BORDER STATE, IN THE BATTLE OF ANTIETAM. UNION TROOPS PUSHED THEM BACK.
THIS WAS THE KIND OF VICTORY FOR WHICH LINCOLN HAD BEEN WAITING.

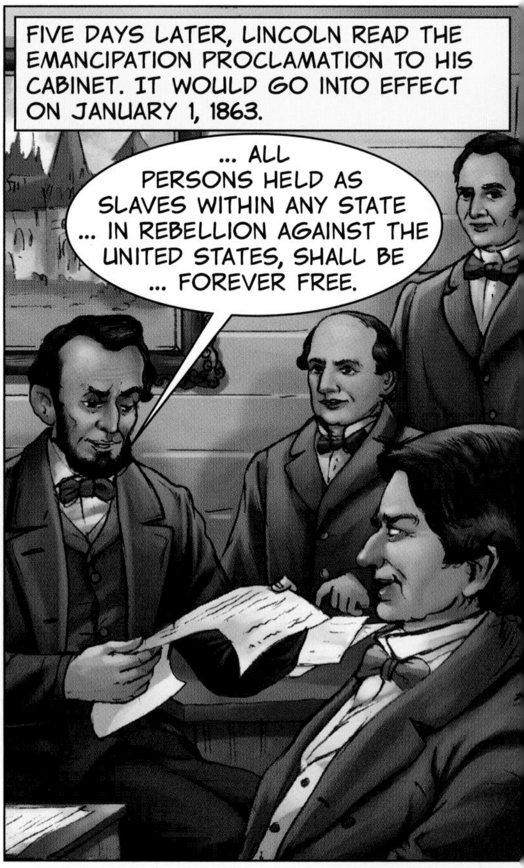
FIVE DAYS LATER, LINCOLN READ THE EMANCIPATION PROCLAMATION TO HIS CABINET. IT WOULD GO INTO EFFECT ON JANUARY 1, 1863.
... ALL PERSONS HELD AS SLAVES WITHIN ANY STATE ... IN REBELLION AGAINST THE UNITED STATES, SHALL BE ... FOREVER FREE.

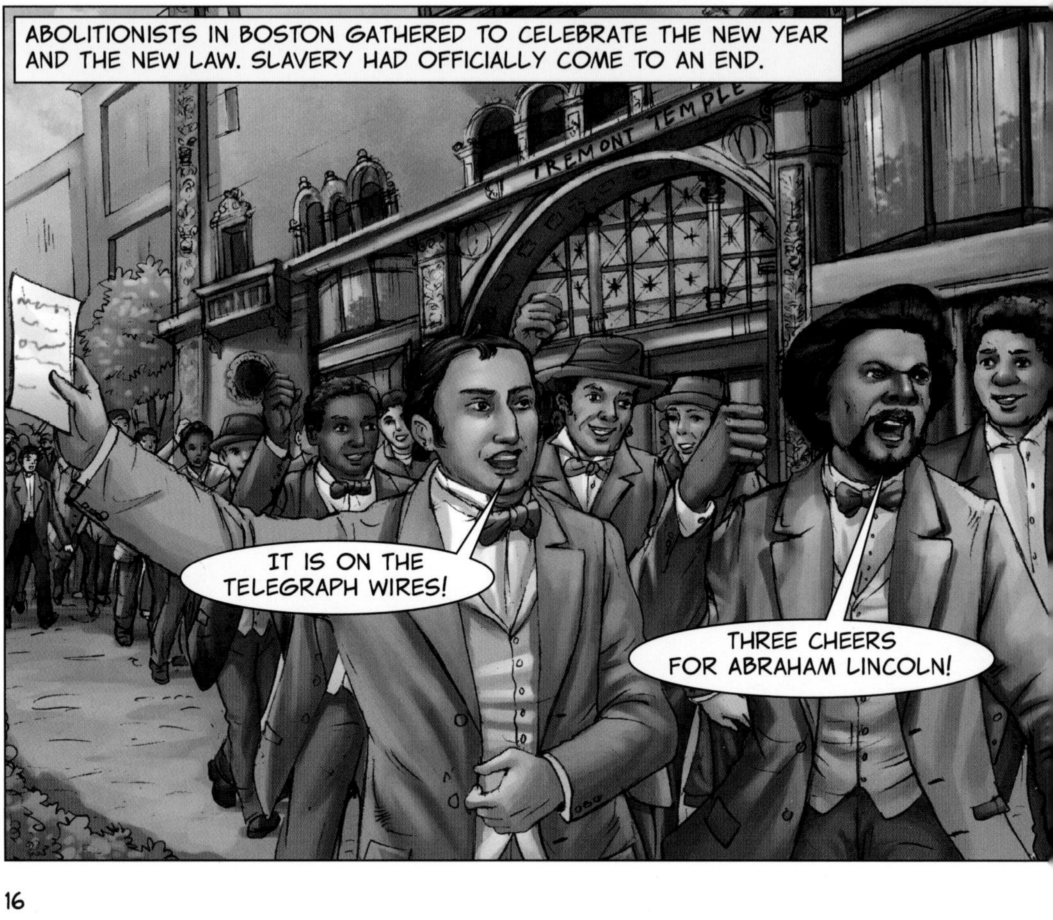
ABOLITIONISTS IN BOSTON GATHERED TO CELEBRATE THE NEW YEAR AND THE NEW LAW. SLAVERY HAD OFFICIALLY COME TO AN END.
TREMONT TEMPLE
IT IS ON THE TELEGRAPH WIRES!
THREE CHEERS FOR ABRAHAM LINCOLN!

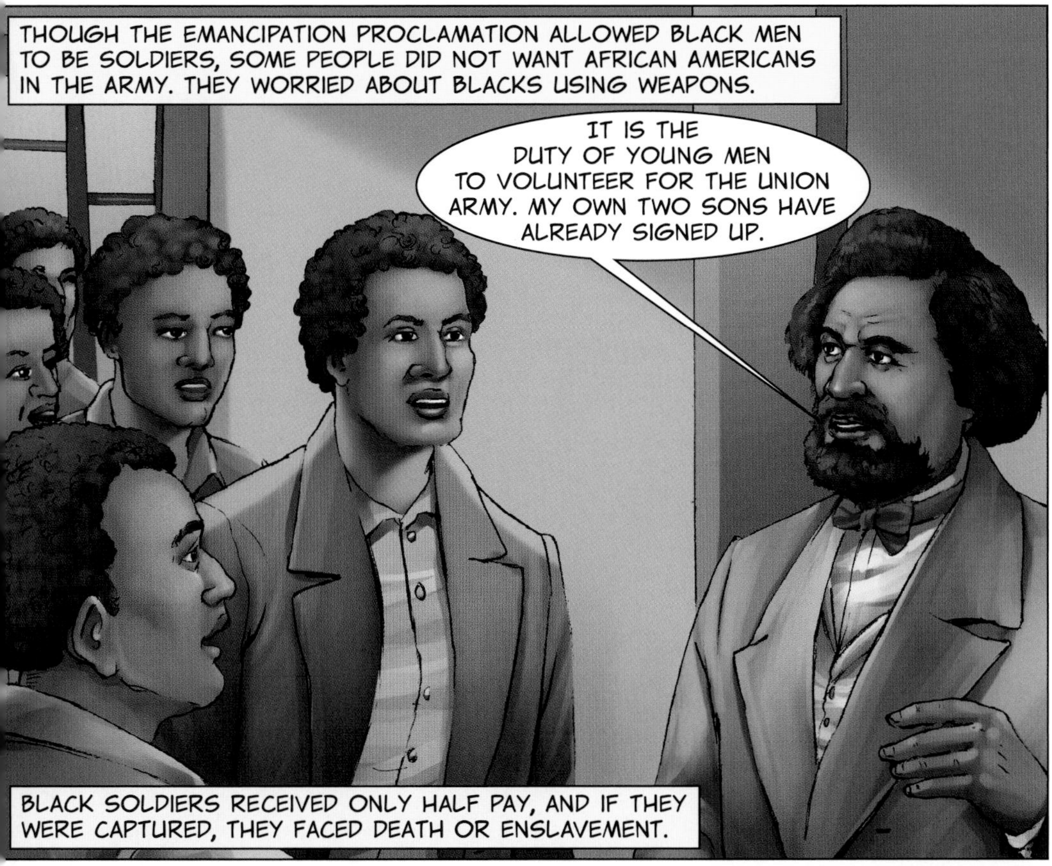
THOUGH THE EMANCIPATION PROCLAMATION ALLOWED BLACK MEN TO BE SOLDIERS, SOME PEOPLE DID NOT WANT AFRICAN AMERICANS IN THE ARMY. THEY WORRIED ABOUT BLACKS USING WEAPONS.
IT IS THE DUTY OF YOUNG MEN TO VOLUNTEER FOR THE UNION ARMY. MY OWN TWO SONS HAVE ALREADY SIGNED UP.
BLACK SOLDIERS RECEIVED ONLY HALF PAY, AND IF THEY WERE CAPTURED, THEY FACED DEATH OR ENSLAVEMENT.

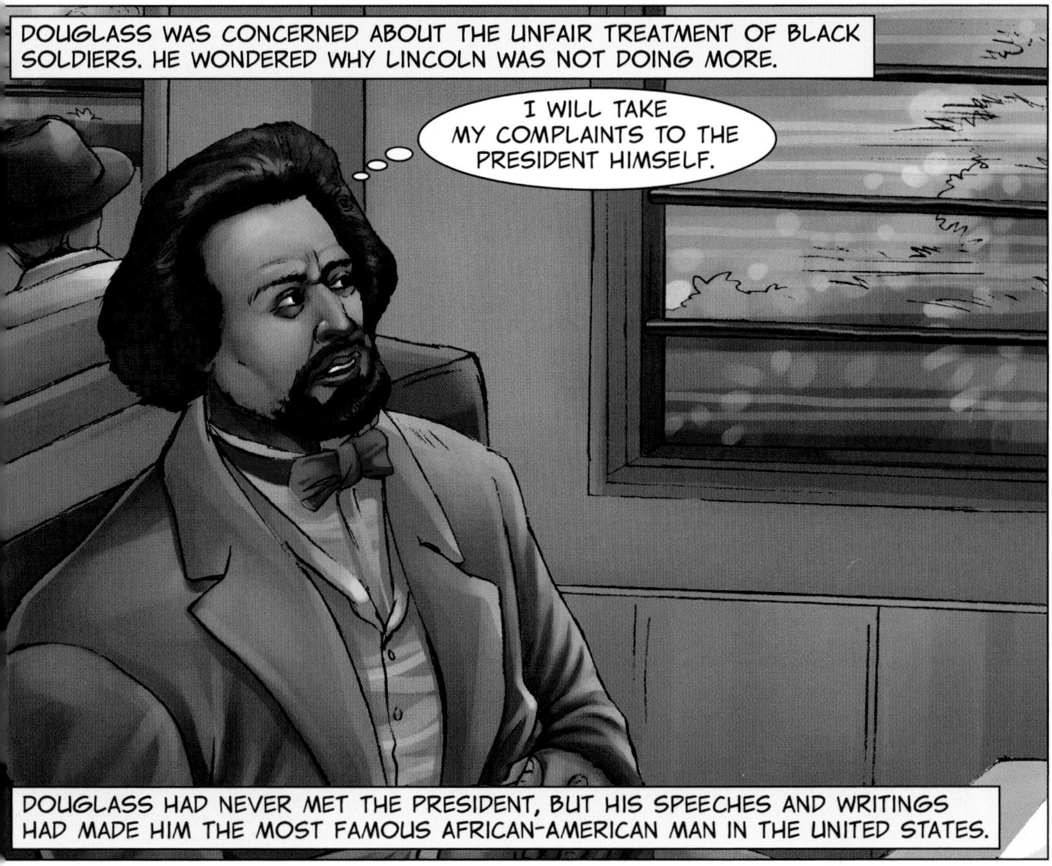
DOUGLASS WAS CONCERNED ABOUT THE UNFAIR TREATMENT OF BLACK SOLDIERS. HE WONDERED WHY LINCOLN WAS NOT DOING MORE.
I WILL TAKE MY COMPLAINTS TO THE PRESIDENT HIMSELF.
DOUGLASS HAD NEVER MET THE PRESIDENT, BUT HIS SPEECHES AND WRITINGS HAD MADE HIM THE MOST FAMOUS AFRICAN-AMERICAN MAN IN THE UNITED STATES.

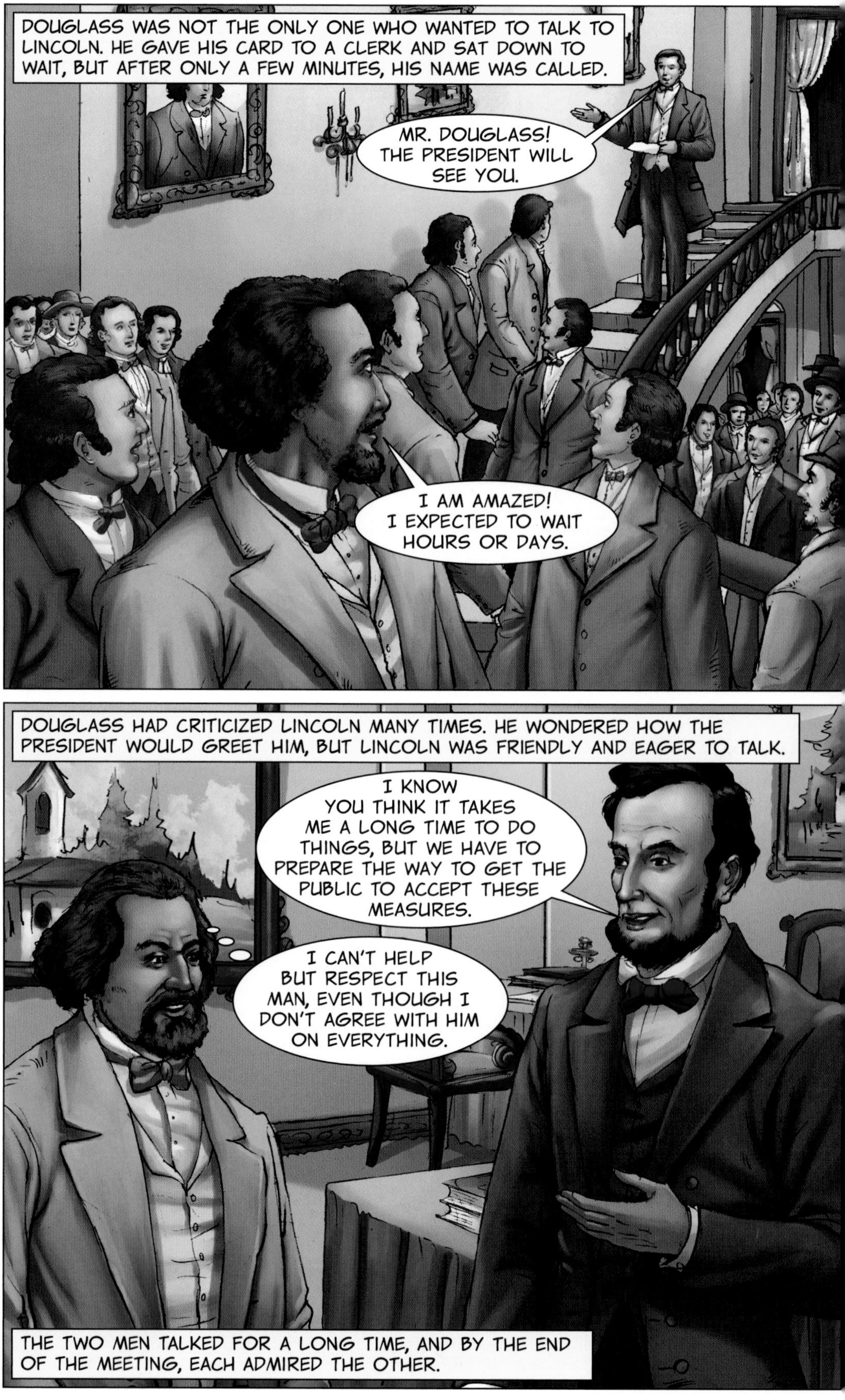
DOUGLASS WAS NOT THE ONLY ONE WHO WANTED TO TALK TO LINCOLN. HE GAVE HIS CARD TO A CLERK AND SAT DOWN TO WAIT, BUT AFTER ONLY A FEW MINUTES, HIS NAME WAS CALLED.
MR. DOUGLASS! THE PRESIDENT WILL SEE YOU.
I AM AMAZED! I EXPECTED TO WAIT HOURS OR DAYS.
DOUGLASS HAD CRITICIZED LINCOLN MANY TIMES. HE WONDERED HOW THE PRESIDENT WOULD GREET HIM, BUT LINCOLN WAS FRIENDLY AND EAGER TO TALK.
I KNOW YOU THINK IT TAKES ME A LONG TIME TO DO THINGS, BUT WE HAVE TO PREPARE THE WAY TO GET THE PUBLIC TO ACCEPT THESE MEASURES.
I CAN'T HELP BUT RESPECT THIS MAN, EVEN THOUGH I DON'T AGREE WITH HIM ON EVERYTHING.
THE TWO MEN TALKED FOR A LONG TIME, AND BY THE END OF THE MEETING, EACH ADMIRED THE OTHER.

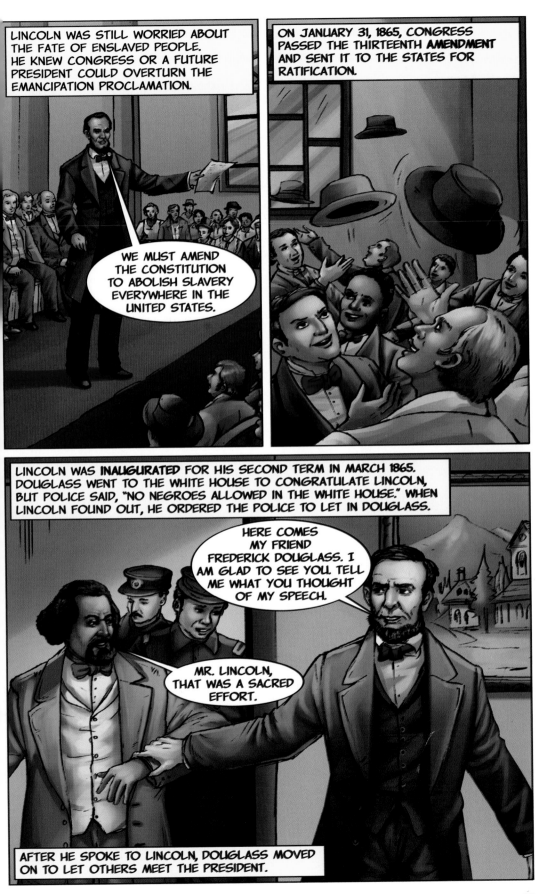

LINCOLN WAS STILL WORRIED ABOUT THE FATE OF ENSLAVED PEOPLE. HE KNEW CONGRESS OR A FUTURE PRESIDENT COULD OVERTURN THE EMANCIPATION PROCLAMATION.

WE MUST AMEND THE CONSTITUTION TO ABOLISH SLAVERY EVERYWHERE IN THE UNITED STATES.

ON JANUARY 31, 1865, CONGRESS PASSED THE THIRTEENTH **AMENDMENT** AND SENT IT TO THE STATES FOR RATIFICATION.

LINCOLN WAS **INAUGURATED** FOR HIS SECOND TERM IN MARCH 1865. DOUGLASS WENT TO THE WHITE HOUSE TO CONGRATULATE LINCOLN, BUT POLICE SAID, "NO NEGROES ALLOWED IN THE WHITE HOUSE." WHEN LINCOLN FOUND OUT, HE ORDERED THE POLICE TO LET IN DOUGLASS.

HERE COMES MY FRIEND FREDERICK DOUGLASS. I AM GLAD TO SEE YOU. TELL ME WHAT YOU THOUGHT OF MY SPEECH.

MR. LINCOLN, THAT WAS A SACRED EFFORT.

AFTER HE SPOKE TO LINCOLN, DOUGLASS MOVED ON TO LET OTHERS MEET THE PRESIDENT.

THE WAR ENDED WITH A UNION VICTORY THE FOLLOWING MONTH, AND LINCOLN WAS ASSASSINATED A FEW DAYS LATER. DOUGLASS FELT THE LOSS DEEPLY. A FEW MONTHS LATER, HE RECEIVED A PACKAGE FROM MARY TODD LINCOLN, THE PRESIDENT'S WIDOW.

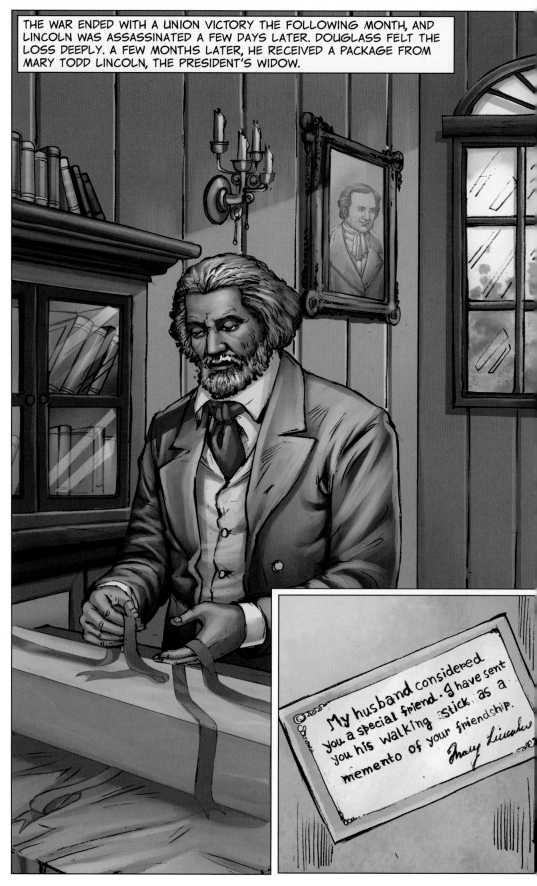

My husband considered you a special friend. I have sent you his walking stick as a memento of your friendship.

Mary Lincoln

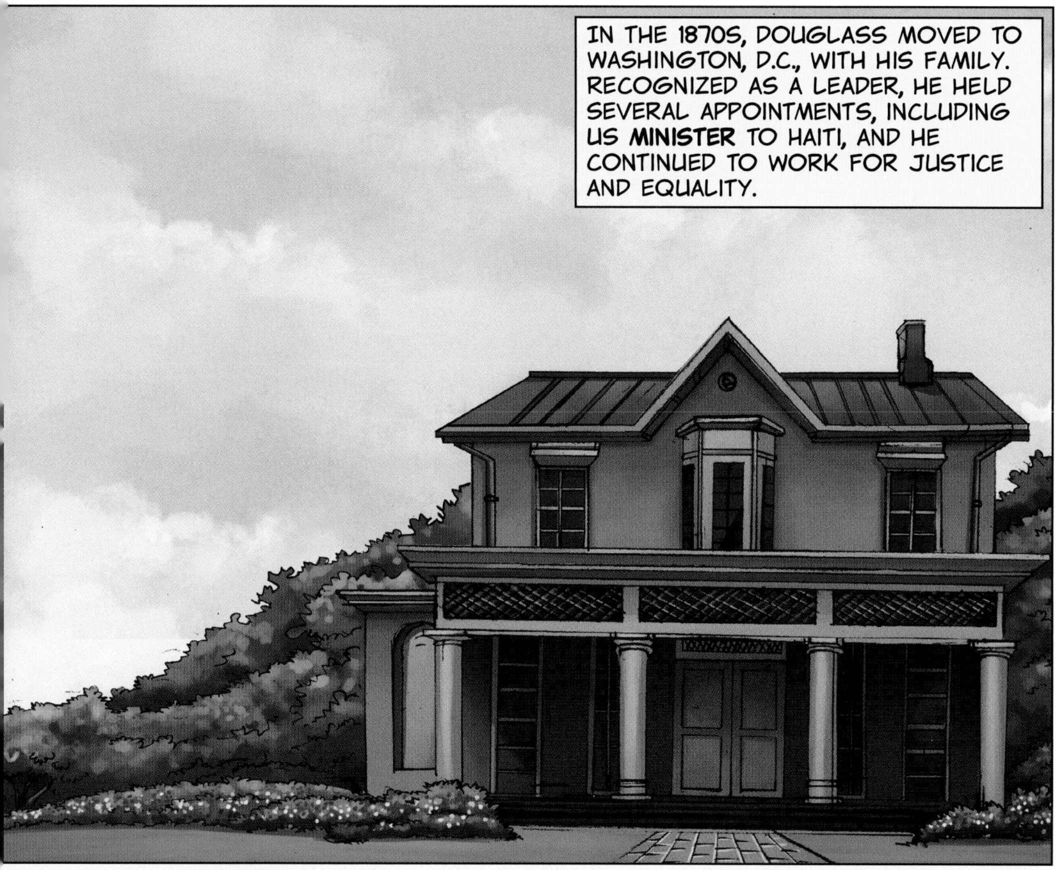
IN THE 1870S, DOUGLASS MOVED TO WASHINGTON, D.C., WITH HIS FAMILY. RECOGNIZED AS A LEADER, HE HELD SEVERAL APPOINTMENTS, INCLUDING US **MINISTER** TO HAITI, AND HE CONTINUED TO WORK FOR JUSTICE AND EQUALITY.

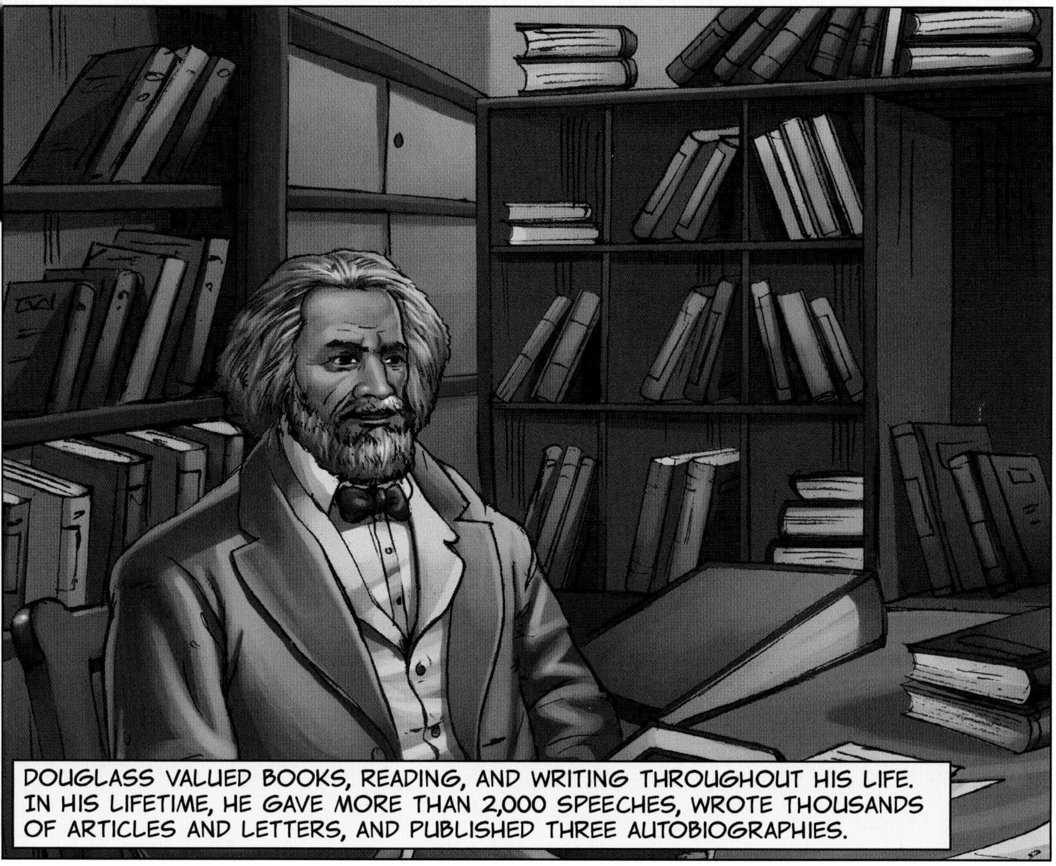
DOUGLASS VALUED BOOKS, READING, AND WRITING THROUGHOUT HIS LIFE. IN HIS LIFETIME, HE GAVE MORE THAN 2,000 SPEECHES, WROTE THOUSANDS OF ARTICLES AND LETTERS, AND PUBLISHED THREE AUTOBIOGRAPHIES.

Timeline

1817 or 1818	Frederick Bailey is born in Talbot County, Maryland.
1826	Frederick is sent to Baltimore to work for Hugh and Sophia Auld.
1837	Frederick joins a club for free black people in Baltimore and meets Anna Murray.
September 3, 1838	Dressed in a borrowed sailor's uniform, Frederick escapes to New York.
September 15, 1838	Frederick and Anna Murray marry. Frederick changes his last name to Douglass.
1841	Douglass speaks at an antislavery meeting in Nantucket and is hired as a speaker.
1845	Douglass publishes his first autobiography, *Narrative of the Life of Frederick Douglass.*
1845–1847	Douglass takes a speaking and fund-raising tour of Britain.
1847	Douglass moves to Rochester, New York, and begins publishing the *North Star.*
1848	Douglass takes part in the first women's rights convention in Seneca Falls, New York.
1851	Douglass's disagreements with William Lloyd Garrison grow.
November 1860	Abraham Lincoln is elected president of the United States.
January 1, 1863	The Emancipation Proclamation takes effect, abolishing slavery in states fighting against the Union.
February 1863	Douglass urges African-American men to fight for the Union.
April 14, 1865	Lincoln is assassinated.
December 18, 1865	The Thirteenth Amendment is ratified, and slavery is outlawed in the United States.
1872	Douglass and his family move to Washington, D.C.
1881	President Garfield appoints Douglass recorder of deeds for the District of Columbia.
1882	Anna Murray Douglass dies.
1884	Douglass marries Helen Pitts.
1889	Douglass is appointed US minister to the Republic of Haiti.
February 20, 1895	Douglass dies of a heart attack after a speech to the National Council of Women.

Glossary

abolitionist (a-buh-LIH-shun-ist) A person who worked to end slavery.

advisers (ed-VY-zurz) People who help you make decisions.

amendment (uh-MEND-ment) An addition or a change to the Constitution.

autobiography (ah-toh-by-AH-gruh-fee) The story of a person's life written by that person.

clergymen (KLUR-jee-men) The people with official duties in a church.

Constitution (kon-stih-TOO-shun) The basic rules by which the United States is governed.

discrimination (dis-krih-muh-NAY-shun) Treating a person badly or unfairly just because he or she is different.

emancipate (ih-MAN-sih-payt) To free from the restraint, control, or power of another, usually referring to the freeing of slaves.

enslaved (en-SLAYVD) Held as a slave.

inaugurated (ih-NAW-gyuh-rayt-ed) Sworn into office.

minister (MIH-nuh-ster) A person who goes to a foreign land on behalf of his or her country.

movement (MOOV-ment) A group of people who get together to support the same cause or goal.

proclamation (prah-kluh-MAY-shun) An official, public announcement.

prosperity (prah-SPER-ih-tee) The condition of being successful.

secede (sih-SEED) To withdraw from a group or a country.

senators (SEH-nuh-terz) People elected to serve in the law-making part of the US government.

ship caulker (SHIP KAHK-er) A craftsman who filled up the cracks and the gaps of a ship to make it waterproof.

suffrage (SUH-frij) The right of voting.

Underground Railroad (UN-dur-grownd RAYL-rohd) A system set up to help slaves move to freedom in the North.

Index

Websites

Due to the changing nature of Internet links, PowerKids Press has developed an online list of websites related to the subject of this book. This site is updated regularly. Please use this link to access the list:

www.powerkidslinks.com/jgaah/fredd/